Hippo
from Another Planet

Written by Arthur Dorros

Illustrated by Joe Boddy

CelebrationPress

An Imprint of ScottForesman
A Division of HarperCollinsPublishers

He was big, he was gray, he was round.
He was a hippo from another planet. At least
that's what everyone said when he landed in
the middle of town.

"But I'm not really from another planet,"
said Fred. "I just came from Watlandia to
look around."

"You don't look like you're from Watlandia," said one of the local hippos.

Fred did look a little unusual. He was wearing red sunglasses and a bubble helmet.

"And that machine you landed in looks like it's from outer space," said another hippo.

Fred had flown from Watlandia in a flying machine he had built. The machine was big, it was round, and it was yellow. But it did fly. Fred just had a bit of trouble with the landings.

4

"Look at this mess," said Henry the grocer. "Whoever heard of landing on piles of fruit and vegetables?"

"Sorry," said Fred. "I was just trying to land safely."

"Do tomatoes look like a safe place to land?" asked Henry.

"They looked softer than the pineapples," Fred thought. "Here, I'll help you clean up," he said. Fred picked up oranges and pears and apples. While he was piling them, he juggled a few.

"Not the tomatoes!" cried Henry.

Fred put the fruits and vegetables into neat piles—five pears on top of six, four on top of five, three on top of four, two on top of three, and finally, one pear balanced carefully on the very top.

"See how clever he is," said Harriet. "He couldn't be from Watlandia. He must be from outer space."

Say something in outer space talk, Fred,"
said Henry.

"I'm not from outer space! I'm from right
over there, across the lake," said
Fred pointing.

"I didn't know there was another planet so
close," said Harriet.

"It's not another planet," said Fred. "It's
Watlandia. Look, you must have heard of
the dance we do in Watlandia—the
Hippo Spin?"

Fred began to dance, spinning and leaping quickly around on the sidewalk. He did the triple front roll turnaround leap. He followed it with the here-to-there bounce— two leaps forward, two somersaults backwards, and two spins sideways.

"Look!" called Henry to a busload of hippos. "Look at this hippo from another planet!"

As he went spinning sideways, Fred bumped into a ladder. When he bumped the ladder, a can of paint tipped. Green paint covered Fred's head and trickled down his neck and back.

"Aaack!" yelled Fred.

"What an unusual word!" said Harriet. "You see, he really does speak outer space talk!"

13

Fred was too busy trying to get the paint off himself to worry about whether anyone thought he was from outer space. He tried to wipe the paint off his head with a cloth.

"Now he's trying to hide!" said Henry. "He must be shy."

"Wouldn't you be, if you came from another planet?" said Harriet.

14

Hippos came running out of buildings and stores and alleys. Trucks and buses and cars were backed up for miles. Hippos stopped whatever they were doing. Everyone wanted to see the hippo from another planet.

"There he is!" said Henry.

"He's part green and part gray," said one hippo.

"He has four eyes!" said another.

"He speaks a strange language!" said a very old hippo.

"Is he dangerous?" asked someone else.

"Only when he lands on the tomatoes," said Henry.

Just then a drop of rain fell. Splat, right on Fred's nose. Raindrops kept falling, splat, splat, splat. Soon it was pouring on everyone. The paint that was on Fred started to wash away. His glasses fogged and he couldn't see a thing.

19

Fred took off his helmet so he could clean his glasses.

"He doesn't look so strange now," said Harriet.

"He looks just like us," said Henry.

"He doesn't look that strange to me," said a tiny hippo named Elbert.

"I'm not strange," said Fred. "I'm just a hippo from Watlandia."

What do they do in Watlandia when it rains?" asked Elbert.

We go swimming," said Fred.

That's just what we do here!" said Elbert.

It's the perfect thing to do when rain is tickling your ears," said Fred. "Watch, I'll show you."

All of the hippos followed Fred, splooshing and splashing in the lake. Fred led them far across the lake, toward Watlandia. When they got near the other shore, they saw all the other Watlandians swimming. In fact, they were doing the Hippo Spin underwater.

"Fred, you're back!" cried Fred's sister, Edna. "But where did all these other hippos come from?"

23

"Fred laughed. "Would you believe they're from another planet?"